THE GREAT "I AM"

WRITTEN BY CHAWNA RENEE ANDERSON

PHOTOGRAPHY BY CHRISTOPHER T. WARD

THE GREAT "I AM"

WRITTEN BY CHAWNA RENEE ANDERSON

PHOTOGRAPHY BY CHRISTOPHER T. WARD

TRIENNIUM
PUBLISHING, LLC

Permissions may be sought directly from the publisher:
Triennium Publishing, LLC
3165 S. Alma School Rd. #29-267
Chandler, AZ 85248
Email: info@trienniumpublishing.com
You may also complete your request on-line at www.trienniumpublishing.com

LIBRARY OF CONGRESS CATALOGUING IN PUBLICATION DATA
A catalogue record for this publication is available from the Library of Congress
ISBN 0-9776410-0-7
SAN: 2 5 7 – 8 2 5 5

Edited by:
Beth Phillips
Eagle Eye Editor
Web: www.eagleeyeeditor.com

Disclaimer: TRIENNIUM PUBLISHING, LLC reserves the right to revise and make changes to this publication without notice.

This Book is Dedicated to:

-All who mourn and are poor in spirit-

For Jesus says, "Blessed are those who mourn,
for they shall be comforted"
and
"Blessed are the poor in spirit,
for theirs is the kingdom in heaven."

(Matthew 5:4,3)

To: _____

From: _____

GOD DID NOT PROMISE A LIFE WITHOUT PAIN, JOY
WITHOUT SORROW OR SUN WITHOUT RAIN.

BUT GOD DID PROMISE STRENGTH FOR THE DAY,
COMFORT FOR TEARS, A LIGHT FOR THE WAY.

AND FOR ALL WHO BELIEVE IN HIS KINGDOM ABOVE,
GOD ANSWERS THEIR FAITH WITH INFINITE LOVE.
—ANONYMOUS

THE AUTHOR'S ACKNOWLEDGEMENTS

First and foremost I give my thanks and praise to my Heavenly Father. I cannot take any credit for this book beyond my obedience to the One who revealed it to me. I thank you, Lord, for your amazing grace and unconditional love.

I thank God everyday for my precious husband, Jeremiah, and our son, Ian. God has shown us both, without a doubt, the extent of his unfailing love, grace, and blessings. I love you, Pappies and Pickles.

I am so blessed to have been given the family and friends that I have. I don't have the words to express the love and gratitude that I have for my mother, Gwyn; my father, Steve, and his wife, Janille; my grandmother, Bettyann Smith; my husband's family: Aaron, Joyce, Travis, and Gina Anderson; my brothers and sister: Stephen Smith, Clinton Ferguson, and Andrea & Terence Ross; and all my nieces and nephews.

Through all the good, the bad, and the ugly, my best friends have been there with me. I thank God for you and your husbands: Amanda & Edmundo Osorio (God will bless your good works), Shannon & Jason Brady, and Trissi & Chris Walker.

To my village of extended family, I give my thanks to the Smiths, the Goerings, the Fergusons, the Talbots, the Schultzes, the Jarboes, and the Henselmiers. I would also like to say "thank you" to the FUMC of El Cajon family that helped in my beginning steps with Jesus. Though time has passed and circumstances have changed, you have always remained in my heart. Thank you, Art & Joline Holmes, Steve & Vicki Lewis, Bob & Lois Elo, Ray & Judy Bratton, and Bob & Marilyn Akers, and their families.

There are a number of people whom God has used specifically to reveal Himself and His purposes to me: Pastor Deborah Schauer, Pastor Andy Welch, Jean-Claude Beauville Jr. and family, Obi Nwambuonwo, Fredrik & Kathi Bergström, Marisol Popoca, Pure Heart Christian Fellowship of Glendale, AZ, and Christopher T. Ward. I thank God for you all!

Last, but certainly not least I would like to give my sincerest thanks to Max Lucado, LLoyd J. Ogilvie, Philip Yancey, Rick Warren, John Ortberg, Tommy Tenney, Kathy Troccoli, Lee Strobel, Loren Cunningham, Henry T. Blackaby and Claude V. King. Your books were a lifeline of hope for me in my darkest hours, a voice of one calling in the desert. (Isa. 40:3) I thank God for every one of you whom God has placed strategically in my life.

THE PHOTOGRAPHER'S ACKNOWLEDGEMENTS

First and foremost, I would like to take this opportunity to thank God for all of the gifts he has given me as well as for providing the opportunities in which all images are created. It is a simple fact that He has provided all of the circumstances in which these photographs were taken; I've merely been blessed enough to be there to click the shutter. None of this would have been possible without God's ever-present Love, Wisdom, and Grace.

I would like to give many special thanks to the following very special people: to my son for his understanding and love - I dedicate this book to you, son; to my mom not only for her love but for kindling the spark of my imagination and sharing her passions for photography and the arts when I was young; to my dad for teaching me to respect the vast beauty of the great outdoors and for taking me to many places that not many people can say they've been; to my oldest brother, Dan, for influencing my love for aviation and for being someone to look up to; to my older brother Mark, who left us far too early yet had a great influence on who I am today; to my little brother, Jon, for all the fun we had growing up together and for his continued companionship and support.

I would like to express my deepest appreciation to everyone who made this book and the photographs within it possible, including very special thanks to: my best friends and confidants Jeremy and Brooks Wolfe, their son Connor, and their daughter Kayla; Lissa and Peter Shigo, and their daughter Sheridan; John and Judy Hogue; Jon Melby; Sean and Erica Mackey; Brian and Carla Streng; Michael and Barbra Wolfe; Ashley and Angus Scott; Stephen Ford; African Bible Colleges and the entire Chinchen clan; Irving Mawolo; Blessings Chikakula; Richard Ebiju; Alex Kikumu; David Kalega; Beth Phillips of Eagle Eye Editor; Chad Rosenthal of HX Book Printing; Jason Hogue of Hogue Printing Solutions; and of course, Chawna for her vision and for allowing me to be a part of it.

Years before I was saved by God's Grace, He introduced me to a very special person who would play a key role in my discovery of Him. She gave me my first Bible, encouraged me to seek Him, and stood with me in 1997 when I photographed the image that adorns the cover of THE GREAT "I AM". Jen, thank you for everything that you have done for my family and me.

THE GREAT "I AM"

LONG AGO, DEEP IN THE WILDERNESS OF EGYPT, GOD APPEARED TO A MAN NAMED MOSES WITHIN THE FLAMES OF A FIRE BURNING IN A BUSH. A FIRE WHICH BURNED IN THE BUSH YET DID NOT CONSUME IT.

GOD SPOKE TO MOSES THAT DAY AND REVEALED HIMSELF AS THE GREAT "I AM". GOD SAID TO MOSES, "I AM WHO I AM. THIS IS WHAT YOU ARE TO SAY TO THE ISREALITES: 'I AM HAS SENT ME TO YOU'. "[1]

GOD STILL SPEAKS TO US TODAY IN MANY WAYS IF WE ARE WILLING TO LISTEN.

THIS IS THE STORY OF THE GREAT "I AM"!

BUT HOW CAN THEY CALL ON HIM
TO SAVE THEM UNLESS THEY BELIEVE IN HIM? AND HOW CAN THEY
BELIEVE IN HIM IF THEY HAVE NEVER HEARD ABOUT HIM? AND
HOW CAN THEY HEAR ABOUT HIM UNLESS SOMEONE TELLS THEM?

(ROMANS 10:14 NLT)

DESPERATE FOR AN ANSWER?

HAS THERE EVER BEEN A TIME IN YOUR LIFE WHEN YOU WERE DESPERATE FOR AN ANSWER? A moment when you were crying out for help, when your heart, mind, and soul needed more than anything else in the world a gift of healing, joy, forgiveness, understanding, and love? Have you ever been buried under the heavy burdens of anger, doubt, resentment, or sorrow? How about perfectionism, addiction, pride, guilt, or worry? Have you ever been completely helpless to change a situation on your own? We have all felt and experienced these miserable truths in our lives. These demons have attacked us all. Yet by God's amazing grace and power we can be set free from their control.

Unfortunately, I know that, for some of you these awful demons are still controlling and deceiving you right now. Binding and choking you so that you can't enjoy life the way God has planned for you: a life filled with an inner joy and peace that can't be destroyed by external factors. You might have given up the fight; you might even be used to the demons. You probably figured there was no answer to your misery and grief.

THERE IS AN ANSWER. There is hope. It is never too late. There is someone far greater than yourself who will strengthen you and fight for you if you let Him. Have you suffered the loss of a loved one, a child's illness, a manipulating addiction, heartbreaking anguish, unexpected changes, a serious disappointment, a broken relationship, or a devastating diagnosis? Do you sometimes feel like you can't go on, as though there's no point? Have you ever wondered if God is with you, if He cares, and if He even hears your cries for help? I believe that, if you look, you just might see that even if you didn't ask, amazingly you made it through another day. Surprisingly, you had the strength to take another step. Wondrously, you were filled with peace. Unexpectedly, an opportunity arose. Unbelievably, you witnessed improvement. Delightfully, you held on to a glimmer of hope. And miraculously, you were given one more day to tell about it. That is the power of God. That is God's generous gifts of mercy and grace.

We have all been thrown life's many wicked curve balls and God has stepped in graciously as our pinch hitter. Even when we didn't acknowledge, thank, or recognize Him, GOD HAS ALWAYS REMAINED WITH US. Now that is true love.

During the times in our life when we are struggling, we must not forget the moments when we've been undeniably blessed. This book is for everyone, believers and nonbelievers alike, to help show and remind us all of God's infinite promises of HIS REDEEMING LOVE, FORGIVENESS, UNDESERVED BLESSINGS AND CONSTANT PRESENCE IN OUR LIVES. He comes to us in many forms, ways that are often ignored or unseen. Faith is seeing the invisible, believing the impossible, and receiving the inconceivable.

JUST IMAGINE. At this very moment you have a bundle of priceless gifts awaiting you in the open arms of Christ. Incredible gifts selected especially for you. Blessings beyond your wildest dreams and expectations. Jesus can't wait to flood you with them. HE HAS GIVEN HIS LIFE FOR YOU to receive them. But you must take the initiative to ask Him for these gifts. You must humble yourself. You must have faith: "I tell you the truth, if you have faith as small as a mustard seed, you can say to this mountain, 'Move from here to there' and it will move. Nothing will be impossible for you." (Matthew 17:20) There is one gift in particular that is, without a doubt, the most magnificent gift of all. IT'S THE GIFT OF GOD HIMSELF and His promise of forgiveness and eternal life. God will remain behind you, next to you, within you, and around you, always within your reach. His gaze will remain upon you forever. He will be constantly loving, healing, forgiving, teaching, listening, and answering you. All you must do to receive is believe. How great is that!

I CRIED OUT TO GOD FOR HELP;

I CRIED OUT TO GOD TO HEAR ME.[2] "O GOD, YOU ARE MY GOD, EARNESTLY I SEEK YOU; MY SOUL THIRSTS FOR YOU, MY BODY LONGS FOR YOU.[3] I CALL ON YOU LORD IN MY DISTRESS AND YOU ANSWER ME.[4] LEAD ME INTO THE DESERT AND SPEAK TO MY HEART."[5]

WHO ARE YOU LORD?

Jesus answered, "I am the way and the truth and the life.[6] I am the light of the world.[7] I am the bread of life.[8] I am the first and I am the last.[9] I am the good shepherd. The good shepherd lays down his life for the sheep".[10] I am who I am,[11] Jehovah, Yahweh, and The Great I am.

WHAT DO YOU WANT OF ME?

"I KNOW THE PLANS I HAVE FOR YOU", DECLARES THE LORD.[12] "I HAVE CALLED YOU BY NAME; YOU ARE MINE.[13] BEFORE I FORMED YOU IN THE WOMB I KNEW YOU, BEFORE YOU WERE BORN I SET YOU APART.[14] I AM THE VINE, YOU ARE THE BRANCHES.[15] YOU DID NOT CHOOSE ME, BUT I CHOSE YOU AND APPOINTED YOU TO GO AND BEAR FRUIT - FRUIT THAT WILL LAST.[16] AS THE FATHER HAS LOVED ME, SO HAVE I LOVED YOU. NOW REMAIN IN MY LOVE".[17]

How will I find You?

"I am with you always to the very end of the age.[18] I revealed myself to those who did not ask for me. I was found by those who did not seek me. To a nation that did not call on my name, I said, 'Here I am, Here I am'.[19] Where two or three come together in my name, there I am with them.[20] You will seek me and find me when you seek me with all of your heart. I will be found by you.[21] You will realize that I am in my Father, and you are in me, and I am in you.[22] Then you will call and I will answer; you will cry for help, and I will say, 'Here I am'.[23]

"I AM THE LORD, THE GOD OF ALL MANKIND. IS ANYTHING TOO HARD FOR ME? [24] SO DO NOT FEAR FOR I AM WITH YOU; DO NOT BE DISMAYED FOR I AM YOUR GOD. I WILL STRENGTHEN YOU AND HELP YOU; I WILL UPHOLD YOU WITH MY RIGHTEOUS RIGHT HAND. [25] I AM THE RESURRECTION AND THE LIFE. WHOEVER BELIEVES IN ME SHALL NOT DIE, BUT HAVE ETERNAL LIFE. [26] DON'T BE AFRAID; JUST BELIEVE. [27] AGAIN JESUS ASKS, 'DO YOU TRULY LOVE ME?' [28] THEN TAKE HEART, YOUR FAITH HAS HEALED YOU AND YOUR SINS ARE FORGIVEN." [29]

"I AM"...

...YOUR OVERFLOWING JOYS.

GREATER "I AM"...

...THAN YOUR DEEPEST SORROWS.

"I AM"...

...YOUR ULTIMATE VICTORIES.

GREATER "I AM"...

...THAN YOUR WORST DEFEATS.

"I AM"...

...YOUR PREVAILING STRENGTHS.

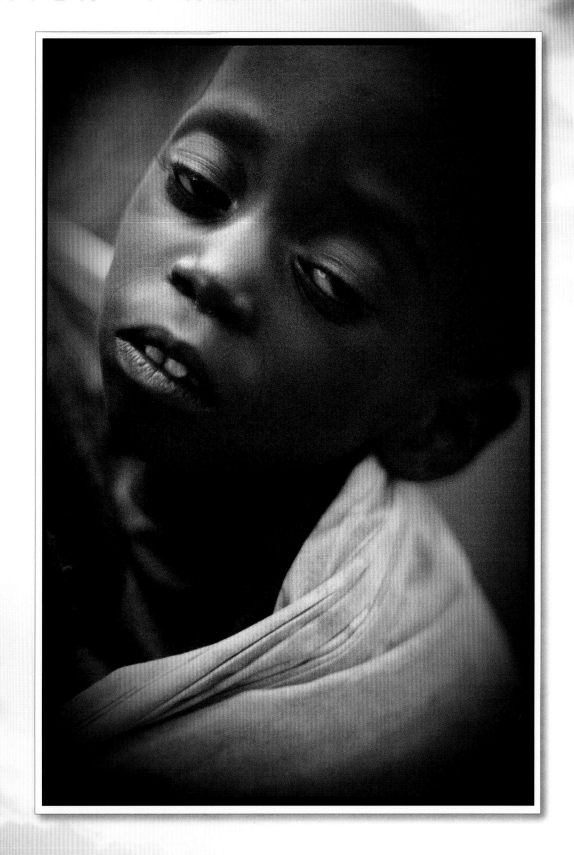

...THAN YOUR EXHAUSTING WEAKNESS.

"I AM"...

...YOUR WONDERFUL COMFORTER.

GREATER "I AM"...

...THAN YOUR TERRIBLE LONELINESS.

"I AM"...

...YOUR UNSTOPPABLE LAUGHTER.

GREATER "I AM"...

...THAN YOUR DESOLATE TEARS.

"I AM"...

...YOUR AMAZING ACCOMPLISHMENTS.

GREATER "I AM"...

...THAN YOUR SADDEST FAILURES.

"I AM"...

...YOUR RELENTLESS AMBITIONS.

GREATER "I AM"...

...THAN YOUR OVERWHELMING LAZINESS.

"I AM"...

...YOUR ONE TRUE LOVE.

GREATER "I AM"...

...THAN YOUR MANY HEART BREAKS.

"I AM"...

...YOUR HEALTHIEST SATISFACTIONS.

GREATER "I AM"...

...THAN YOUR SICKEST TEMPTATIONS.

"I AM"...

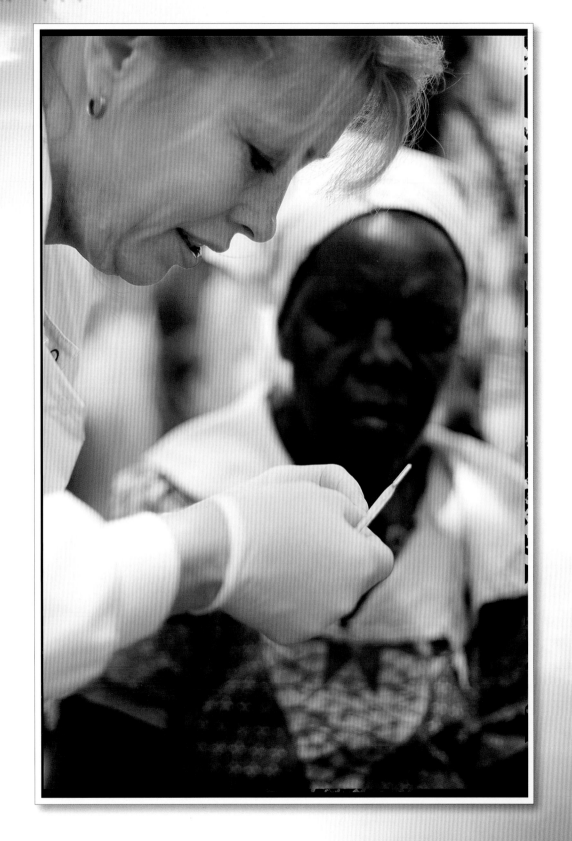

...YOUR MOST TENDER HEALING.

GREATER "I AM"...

...THAN YOUR MEANEST ILLNESS.

"I AM"...

...YOUR ASTOUNDING COURAGE.

GREATER "I AM"...

...THAN YOUR DEVASTATING FEARS.

"I AM"...

...YOUR IMPOSSIBLE DREAMS.

GREATER "I AM"...

...THAN YOUR UNFULFILLED EXPECTATIONS.

"I AM"...

...YOUR GUIDING LIGHT.

GREATER "I AM"...

...THAN YOUR CONSUMING DARKNESS.

"I AM"...

...YOUR THRILLING EXCITEMENT.

GREATER "I AM"...

...THAN YOUR TEDIOUS BOREDOM.

"I AM"...

...YOUR PUREST CLEANSING.

GREATER "I AM"...

...THAN YOUR WORRISOME JUNK.

...THAN YOUR SILLIEST MISTAKES.

"I AM"...

...YOUR ABUNDANT FORGIVENESS.

"I AM" SO MUCH GREATER...

...THAN YOUR ENDLESS SINS.

TRUST ME, FOR "I AM"...

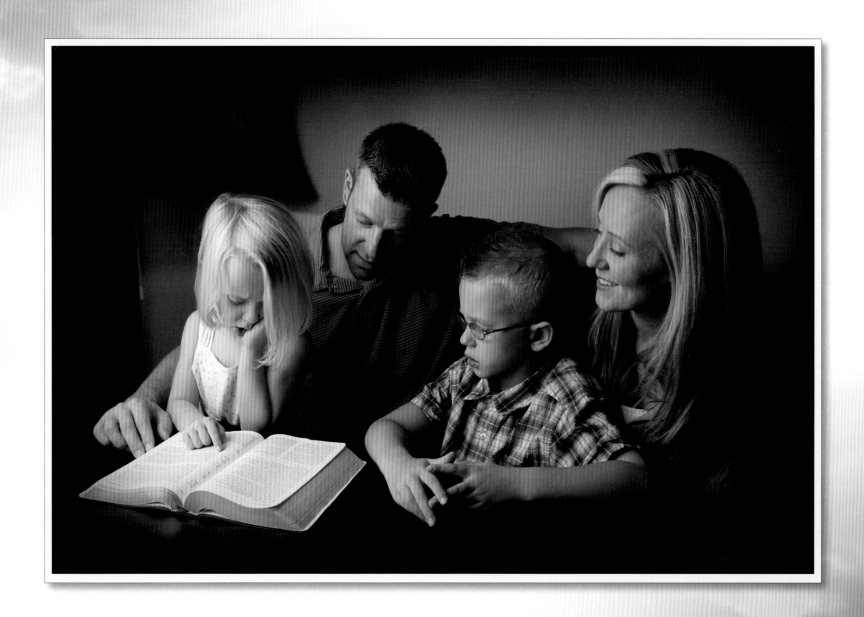

...THE SIMPLEST SOLUTION TO YOUR MOST COMPLEX PROBLEMS.

I LOVE AND RESPECT YOU DEEPLY.

THAT IS WHY I HAVE GIVEN YOU THE FREE WILL TO DECIDE
HOW GREAT "I AM" TO YOU.

"I HAVE LOVED YOU,"

SAYS THE LORD. [30] "I AM THE LORD YOUR GOD, WHO TEACHES YOU WHAT IS BEST FOR YOU AND DIRECTS YOU IN THE WAY YOU SHOULD GO. [31] I AM WITH YOU AND WILL SAVE YOU. [32] THEREFORE I TELL YOU, DO NOT WORRY ABOUT YOUR LIFE, WHAT YOU WILL EAT OR DRINK; OR ABOUT YOUR BODY WHAT YOU WILL WEAR. [33] ASK AND IT WILL BE GIVEN TO YOU; SEEK AND YOU WILL FIND; KNOCK AND THE DOOR WILL BE OPENED. [34] I HAVE LOVED YOU WITH AN EVERLASTING LOVE; I HAVE DRAWN YOU WITH LOVING KINDNESS. [35] I WILL RESTORE YOU TO HEALTH AND HEAL YOUR WOUNDS. [36] SO YOU WILL BE MY PEOPLE AND I WILL BE YOUR GOD." [37]

"BUT WHAT ABOUT YOU?"
JESUS ASKS. "WHO DO YOU SAY I AM?"
(MATTHEW 16:15)

DO NOT BE ANXIOUS ABOUT ANYTHING,

BUT IN EVERYTHING, BY PRAYER AND PETITION, WITH THANKSGIVING, PRESENT YOUR REQUESTS TO GOD. AND THE PEACE OF GOD, WHICH TRANSCENDS ALL UNDERSTANDING, WILL GUARD YOUR HEARTS AND YOUR MINDS IN CHRIST JESUS.

(PHILIPPIANS 4:6-7)

PRAYER OF ACCEPTANCE:

"For God so loved the world that he gave his one and only Son, that whoever believes in him shall not perish but have eternal life."
(John 3:16)

If you have never accepted Jesus Christ as your Lord and Savior, and are unsure of where you will spend eternity, if you want to lay your life and burdens at the feet of Christ, then say this prayer from your heart...

"Jesus, I am a sinner. Please forgive me. Please enter into my heart and my life and make me into a new creation. Fill me with your Holy Spirit. I thank you for loving me so much that you gave up your own life to save mine. I give you my life, Lord, in the name of Jesus Christ, the only name by which I am saved. Amen"

If you want to know more about how to have a personal relationship with Jesus, you can talk with someone right now by calling 1-888-needhim or visiting online at www.needhim.org

As soon as Jesus was baptized, he went up out of the water. At that moment heaven was opened, and he saw the Spirit of God descending like a dove and lighting on him. And a voice from heaven said, "This is my Son, whom I love; with him I am well pleased."

(Matthew 3:16-17)

AND THIS WATER SYMBOLIZES BAPTISM THAT NOW SAVES YOU ALSO — NOT THE REMOVAL OF DIRT FROM THE BODY
BUT THE PLEDGE OF A GOOD CONSCIENCE TOWARD GOD. IT SAVES YOU BY THE RESURRECTION OF JESUS CHRIST,

(1 PETER 3:21)

"COME, FOLLOW ME,"
JESUS SAID, "AND I WILL MAKE YOU FISHERS OF MEN."
(MARK 1:17)

THE PHOTOGRAPHS:

The following pages contain thumbnails of the photographs that are included within *THE GREAT "I AM."* Each thumbnail is accompanied by a description which explains its relation to the page on which it appears and a reference to Scripture that gives meaning to the page. The photographs span much of my career as a professional photographer as well as some years before I turned pro.

Many of the photographs come from my involvement in short-term missions trips to Africa. In 2004 I traveled with a 27-member short-term missions team from Canyon Ridge Bible Church, to Malawi, a country in Africa, where we supported the African Bible College (ABC) in Lilongwe. The team members were organized into a medical team, a construction team, a children-and-orphanage-ministry team, a music-ministry team, and a sports-ministry team. I was fortunate enough to be able to accompany each of the ministry teams at one point or another as they did their work, a situation which gave me the opportunities to capture some of the photographs you see here.

In May 2005, I traveled alone to Uganda, Africa, on another short-term missions trip to support the construction of ABC's newest campus in Kampala. I made friends with many of the men with whom I worked closely on building the new campus. Classes started at the new Uganda Campus in September 2005, and I am proud to have been there to help make that happen. The students that graduate from African Bible College, and other missions organizations like it, bring hope to the future of a continent that has been ravaged by civil war, poverty, and disease.

It is my hope that these photographs and the stories behind them have spurred your interest in missions trips. Missions organizations around the world rely on people like you and me to send support not only in the form of donations of goods and money but also in the form of people who are willing to travel to a foreign land to lend a hand. Short-term missions provide many opportunities and experiences that you will treasure for life. You don't need a particular skill, just a good heart and willingness to work in the name of Jesus Christ.

One of our goals for *THE GREAT "I AM"* is that it will be used to gather support for ministries and missions in the effort to spread the hope and freedom found within Jesus Christ and to share it with the rest of the world.

DO YOU SEE HIM?

BUT HOW CAN THEY CALL ON HIM

TO SAVE THEM UNLESS THEY BELIEVE IN HIM? AND HOW CAN THEY BELIEVE IN HIM IF THEY HAVE NEVER HEARD ABOUT HIM? AND HOW CAN THEY HEAR ABOUT HIM UNLESS SOMEONE TELLS THEM?

(ROMANS 10:14 NLT)

LOST IN THE FIRE - FOUND IN ITS RUINS
(Photograph preceding page)

Arizona is home to some of the southwest's most pristine Sonoran Desert, which teems with the region's unique native plant life. In 1995, the Rio Fire swept through a large part of the desert north of Scottsdale, and after wiping out more than 25,000 acres of saguaro cactus, brittlebush, palo verde and other native trees, plants, and wildflowers, the fire left in its wake an eerie graveyard of charred remains. In early 1996, I went mountain biking with my brother Jon and a friend in an area of desert that the fire had swept through. I was immediately drawn to the ruins the fire had left behind—a landscape like no other I had ever seen before. I became fascinated with this place and traveled there many times, both on my mountain bike and on foot with camera in hand to capture it on film.

On my second trip to the area I found an unusually beautiful place where a great saguaro had once stood. I was intrigued not only with the great icon that had once towered as one of the largest saguaros in the area but also with the location and its surroundings of bouldered hills and fallen trees. The saguaro, once probably 40 feet tall, was now just a 15-foot-tall skeleton that had a cross-like appearance. Nearby was a palo verde tree that had also succumbed to the fire. Its once-green bark was completely burned off, and the skeleton that remained was now smooth, gray, and rustic looking. Though it was now a lifeless hulk left behind by the fire, its geometry and shape of its branches were still perfect and a very striking image to the eye. The beauty of this tree captured my photographic curiosity, and I took many photographs of it, experimenting with new angles and light each time I visited. In late 1997 I captured the photograph of the palo verde as you see it on the preceding page. When the film came back from the lab and I saw the colors of the sky behind the stunning silhouette of the lifeless tree, I knew I had something special. It would take four years, however, for me to find out how special.

In 2001 I featured this photograph as a 20-by-30-inch framed print at the Scottsdale Arts Festival, and during the three days of the show, many people would stop to look at it and spend many moments pointing out different shapes that they saw in the image. One shape that I heard about all weekend was the silhouette of a woman in the tree's trunk, and by the end of the show I had grown tired of answering the question "Have you ever noticed the figure in this picture?" Near the end of the last day of the show, a young couple came by my booth and spent what seemed like 10 minutes in front of the photograph staring at it. I could hear them whispering back and forth, but I was accustomed to this by now and didn't pay much attention to them.

Then came the question. "Have you ever noticed things in this photograph?" the young man asked. I answered yes and told him of the figure in the tree trunk that so many people had pointed out. He then said, "Yeah, we saw that too, but have you ever seen the face in the clouds?"

"Face in the clouds?" I asked as I stood up. "No, I haven't." I walked over to where the couple stood and the young man pointed to the photograph.

"Look. Here in the clouds where these two branches make a circle is a face: here are the eyes, his nose, and his mouth." As I looked where he pointed, the face immediately appeared to me. I was amazed. Since that day, I cannot look at that photograph without looking directly into the face that peers back at me out of the clouds.

As I look back at the experience of being shown the face in the clouds in this image, I can say that the experience very much parallels my experience of finding God. Knowledge often precedes understanding, and sometimes it takes someone else to help point out the obvious. I would never have come to know God if it weren't for the many people in my life who pointed Him out to me. Now that I have a relationship with Jesus Christ, I now know that God has always been there casting His light to guide my way, picking me up when I have fallen, and creating circumstances and opportunities in my life which are otherwise inexplicable.

Since starting this project, Chawna and I have both had experiences that have no explanation other than God having His hand and purpose behind it, and the purpose behind many of my experiences is now clear. At those times I often considered myself lucky when, in reality, God was bestowing His blessings upon me. Though my family was not "religious" during my childhood, I can remember thinking about God in wonder since I was very young, and now I know it was "understanding" and "belief" that had eluded me. I believe we are all born with the knowledge of God, but it is up to us to discover and understand His unconditional, everlasting love and grace.

I like to think that God was speaking to me on that day back in 1997, and if you look close you can see His words: the Light of the world.

[signature]

(Lost In The Fire – Found In Its Ruins, Scottsdale, Arizona - October 1997)

I CRIED OUT TO GOD FOR HELP.

Communication is an essential part of any relationship. Without it we lose touch and become isolated from those that we share our lives with. It is only natural that daily prayer is a fundamental part of our relationship with God. The Lord longs to hear from you every minute of everyday. He has so much that He wants to share with you as well. Through Scripture we are called to pray throughout our daily lives.
~Chawna Anderson
(Taylor Ward walks across the face of a large dune at the Coral Pink Sand Dune State Park in Utah - July 2001.)

I RISE BEFORE DAWN AND CRY FOR HELP; I HAVE PUT MY HOPE IN YOUR WORD. (PSALM 119:147)

WHO ARE YOU LORD?

Knowing God in all of His splendor and majesty is humanly impossible. His character is flawless and His beauty, incomprehensible. Let us spend a lifetime seeking Him, that we may get a glimpse of His Glory.
~ Chawna Anderson
 (First light at the Tetons. Grand Teton National Park, Wyoming - July 1998.)

JESUS SAID TO THEM, "COME AND HAVE BREAKFAST. " NONE OF THE DISCIPLES DARED ASK HIM, "WHO ARE YOU?" THEY KNEW IT WAS THE LORD. (JOHN 21:12)

WHAT DO YOU WANT OF ME?

This photograph is of a beautiful woman named Tineque Woods. When she was three months pregnant with her second child, her husband was killed in an act of violence. Six months later and a week after this photo was taken she had a precious baby girl. Tineque is currently raising her two daughters Alanna and Amaya, and is working as a case manager with the mentally ill.
~ Chawna Anderson
(Tineque Woods stands in an orange grove for THE GREAT "I AM" - March 2003.)

IN HIM WE WERE ALSO CHOSEN, HAVING BEEN PREDESTINED ACCORDING TO THE PLAN OF HIM WHO WORKS OUT EVERYTHING IN CONFORMITY WITH THE PURPOSE OF HIS WILL. (EPHESIANS 1:11)

HOW WILL I FIND YOU?

Are you praying for someone who is lost? Take comfort, for our Heavenly Father knows exactly where they are. Pray that their spiritual eyes will be opened, so that they may call out to God to be found.
~Chawna Anderson
(A view of the road to Clappers Flat near Laurel, Montana - January 2005.)

"ASK AND IT WILL BE GIVEN TO YOU; SEEK AND YOU WILL FIND; KNOCK AND THE DOOR WILL BE OPENED TO YOU. FOR EVERYONE WHO ASKS RECEIVES; HE WHO SEEKS FINDS; AND TO HIM WHO KNOCKS, THE DOOR WILL BE OPENED. " (MATTHEW 7:7-8)

CAN YOU HELP ME?

When Jesus Christ was crucified at Calvary, the eternal battle against Satan was won on that day. It is our choice whether we accept God's hand in our personal daily battles against the evil one's attacks, and it is only with His help that we can claim victory against Satan in Jesus' name.
~ Chawna Anderson
(Digital composite created for *THE GREAT "I AM"* - April 2004.)

GOD IS OUR REFUGE AND STRENGTH, AN EVER-PRESENT HELP IN TROUBLE. (PSALM 46:1)

OVERFLOWING JOYS

There is no purer joy than that within a young child. Children smile, laugh, and squeal regardless of the circumstances around them. A child's joy overflows to all who witness it. If we choose to trust in God, rather than in our circumstances, we too could experience a joy and peace that surpasses all understanding.
~ Chawna Anderson
(Sheridan Shigo plays in a flag for this photo which was taken for her parents, Lissa and Peter Shigo – July 2002.)

MAY THE GOD OF HOPE FILL YOU WITH ALL JOY AND PEACE AS YOU TRUST IN HIM, SO THAT YOU MAY OVERFLOW WITH HOPE BY THE POWER OF THE HOLY SPIRIT. (ROMANS 15:13)

DEEPEST SORROWS

In 1982, my older brother Mark was killed in a car accident at the age of just 20. He was far too young when he left us, and the loss affected all of us but no one more than my mother. From my experience, I can say that the loss of a loved one puts a great strain on a family. That strain can create a crack which can then become a void in the relationships of those that are left behind. Such a loss can change you to your core, and life definitely changed for all of us the day Mark was taken. The sorrow of losing Mark still affects my mother; she still often openly grieves for her son. When I think about Mark, it seems as if I hardly knew him, yet without his influence I would not be the same person I am today. The things that I looked up to in Mark became things that I enjoy to this day, such as weightlifting and cycling. I asked my mother to share her thoughts, and this is what she said: "The loss of a child is the most unbearable thing that can happen to a mother. The sense of loss envelopes the world, swallows the future, and never goes away. The loss becomes manageable and you learn to go on, but the loss of a child is forever a hole in your life."
~ Christopher T. Ward
(Sharon Ward holds a portrait of her son, my brother Mark Ward – November 2005.)

THEN MAIDENS WILL DANCE AND BE GLAD, YOUNG MEN AND OLD AS WELL. I WILL TURN THEIR MOURNING INTO GLADNESS; I WILL GIVE THEM COMFORT AND JOY INSTEAD OF SORROW. (JEREMIAH 31:13)

ULTIMATE VICTORIES

The taste of victory is sweet, and it is even sweeter when we are victorious in the face of overbearing circumstances when all seems lost. If we are willing to let God take the reins of our lives during such circumstances, he can lead us through them and on to our ultimate victories. Have you praised God for your ultimate victories?
~Christopher T. Ward
(Jeremy Wolfe races for the finish line in this film composite created for *THE GREAT "I AM"* - May 2005.)

FOR EVERYONE BORN OF GOD OVERCOMES THE WORLD. THIS IS THE VICTORY THAT HAS OVERCOME THE WORLD, EVEN OUR FAITH. (1 JOHN 5:4)

Worst Defeats

When we are faced with a challenge and defeated, there is only one thing we can do to claim victory: praise God, then get up and keep fighting.
~ Chawna Anderson
(Digital composite created for *THE GREAT "I AM"* - September 2004.)

BROTHERS, I DO NOT CONSIDER MYSELF YET TO HAVE TAKEN HOLD OF IT. BUT ONE THING I DO: FORGETTING WHAT IS BEHIND AND STRAINING TOWARD WHAT IS AHEAD, I PRESS ON TOWARD THE GOAL TO WIN THE PRIZE FOR WHICH GOD HAS CALLED ME HEAVENWARD IN CHRIST JESUS. (PHILIPIANS 3:13-14)

Prevailing Strengths

Doress Robert and her child Chinsinsi Robert sit in the doorway of their home in the small village of Chigowo just outside of Lilongwe, Malawi. Doress had just come with her baby from the fields where she was plowing rows for corn using her hands and the spiked, bat-like tool she is holding in the photograph. In the villages of Malawi, the women care for their children while working in the fields, fetching water, gathering wood, and cooking. You can imagine that such responsibility takes great strength. Where do you get your strength?
~ Christopher T. Ward
(Doress and Chinsinsi Robert, Chigowo Village, Malawi, Africa - June 2004.)

"THE LORD IS MY STRENGTH AND MY SONG; HE HAS BECOME MY SALVATION. HE IS MY GOD, AND I WILL PRAISE HIM, MY FATHER'S GOD, AND I WILL EXALT HIM. " (EXODUS 15:2)

Exhausting Weakness

During my trip to Malawi in 2004, I was fortunate enough to accompany most of the outreach teams at one time or another while they did their work in various locations. One of the main jobs of the medical team was to go to the Kangaonde village to care for the people there. During our visit, this 3-year-old girl named Grace M'bwayuka was discovered to be very malnourished and sick. Though she was three, she could not walk and was on her mother's back when I took this photo. With her mother's blessing, the medical team decided that Grace would come back to the African Bible College, where she would get better treatment in the medical clinic there.

Upon our return to the African Bible College it was discovered that Grace's complications came from HIV, which had been passed on to her from her mother. Unfortunately, the day after we brought Grace to the ABC, she passed away as a result of complications from AIDS. Her father had already succumbed to the disease almost a year earlier, and eight months after Grace passed away, her mother followed. Many countries on the continent of Africa including Malawi are in a fierce battle with the AIDS pandemic.
~ Christopher T. Ward
(Weak and dying, Grace M'bwayuka rests on her mother's back. Kangaonde village, Malawi, Africa – June 2004.)

TO THE WEAK I BECAME WEAK, TO WIN THE WEAK. I HAVE BECOME ALL THINGS TO ALL MEN SO THAT BY ALL POSSIBLE MEANS I MIGHT SAVE SOME. (I CORINTHIANS 9:22)

Wonderful Comforter

There is nothing more comforting than a loving embrace from your mother and father. Our Father in heaven longs to wrap His arms around us and comfort us in our times of need.
~ Chawna Anderson
(Sheridan Shigo is comforted for this photograph by her mother and father Lissa and Peter Shigo – October 2001.)

SHOUT FOR JOY, O HEAVENS; REJOICE, O EARTH; BURST INTO SONG, O MOUNTAINS! FOR THE LORD COMFORTS HIS PEOPLE AND WILL HAVE COMPASSION ON HIS AFFLICTED ONES. (ISAIAH 49:13)

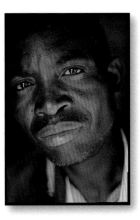

Terrible Loneliness

During my trip to Malawi in 2004, I was asked to travel as an ambassador on behalf of the missions team to meet with the Chief of the Kangaonde village, Sir Tsekulani Kanyoni. Our mission was to ask Chief Kanyoni's permission to bring the medical team there to treat his people. In short, it was one of the most memorable experiences of my lifetime.

Our guide and interpreter, Blessings Chikakula, and I hitchhiked up the main highway to the village trail and then traveled two miles by bicycle taxi to the village. Upon arriving at the outskirts of the village, Blessings halted our progress because a funeral was in session there. After the service concluded and the procession moved on to bury the dead, we cautiously entered the village, where we met with Chief Kanyoni. The chief invited us into his home, a small mud hut with a grass roof, for the meeting. To be so invited is a great privilege according to Malawian customs. We sat on the mud floor of the chief's home and talked to him through Blessings.

The meeting went very well, and permission to bring in the medical team was granted. As we exited the chief's home, I asked Blessings to ask the chief if I could take his portrait. He obliged, and as he stood in front of his door for the portrait, the funeral procession returned from the burial ground and passed just behind me. It was a haunting experience, and as the wailing of the village women marked the procession's time and place, I captured several photos of the chief.

The chief exuded a feeling of loneliness in the portraits I captured of him, and after leaving the village I learned from Blessings that the chief's last wife had died from complications of AIDS just months earlier in December 2003, and his son had died 10 days after birth, an event which was said to have contributed to the mother's death. The chief's third wife and his sister, Nee Nasikelo Kanyoni, also had died in 1999 as a result of AIDS.

When I returned to the village with the medical team the following day, I had the honor of presenting the chief with a portrait which I had printed the previous night. I was amazed to find out that he had never seen a photograph before, let alone a picture of himself. While doing research for THE GREAT "I AM," I was sad to learn that Chief Kanyoni died as a result of AIDS on August 22, 2004, just 2 months after we had visited his village. Seeing firsthand the effects that AIDS has had on the villages of Malawi is something I will never forget, and the image of the lonely chief will forever be a reminder of my experience that day.

~ Christopher T. Ward

(Chief Kanyoni poses for a portrait, Kangoande Village, Malawi, Africa – June 2004.)

A FATHER TO THE FATHERLESS, A DEFENDER OF WIDOWS, IS GOD IN HIS HOLY DWELLING. GOD SETS THE LONELY IN FAMILIES, HE LEADS FORTH THE PRISONERS WITH SINGING; BUT THE REBELLIOUS LIVE IN A SUN-SCORCHED LAND. (PSALM 68:5-6)

Unstoppable Laughter

When you enter a village in Malawi, you can expect to be greeted by a running mob of laughing children. I've never seen such laughter before my visits there. It takes just one youngster to sound the alarm —"AZUNGU!" (meaning "white man" in Chichewa, the native tongue)—and you will find yourself overwhelmed by a crowd of screaming and laughing children, many of which seem to appear out of nowhere.

Malawi is the fourth-poorest country in the world, and though these people may seem to have nothing of value, that couldn't be further from the truth, for it seems they have a genuine happiness that material things cannot fetch.

~ Christopher T. Ward

(The children of Chigowo Village, Malawi, Africa greet me with laughter at the outskirts of their village – June 2004.)

THE RANSOMED OF THE LORD WILL RETURN. THEY WILL ENTER ZION WITH SINGING; EVERLASTING JOY WILL CROWN THEIR HEADS. GLADNESS AND JOY WILL OVERTAKE THEM, AND SORROW AND SIGHING WILL FLEE AWAY. (ISAIAH 51:11)

MISERABLE TEARS

God has promised to turn our sorrows into triumphs. In your time of sorrow, turn to God, for He will restore your fortunes and turn your tears into songs of joy.
~ Chawna Anderson
(Erica Mackey poses in this photograph created for THE GREAT "I AM"- November 2005.)

THOSE WHO SOW IN TEARS WILL REAP WITH SONGS OF JOY. (PSALMS 126:5)

AMAZING ACCOMPLISHMENTS

When my younger brother Steve was three years old, my parents were told that he was mentally challenged and would never be in regular curriculum classes at school, nor would he amount to much in life. He has since graduated from high school in all regular-curriculum classes. At twenty-four years old he moved away from home to go to school to learn auto mechanics. He graduated with a 3.5 GPA and was accepted into a specialized auto-mechanic program.
~ Chawna Anderson
(Steve Smith poses for this photograph created for THE GREAT "I AM" – August 2005.)

FOR EVERYONE BORN OF GOD OVERCOMES THE WORLD. THIS IS THE VICTORY THAT HAS OVERCOME THE WORLD, EVEN OUR FAITH. WHO IS IT THAT OVERCOMES THE WORLD? ONLY HE WHO BELIEVES THAT JESUS IS THE SON OF GOD. (1 JOHN 5:4-5)

SADDEST FAILURES

Failure comes in many forms throughout life, and often it presents itself during some of life's darkest hours through circumstances we cannot control. And though most people consider failure as something to be looked down upon, it is often through our greatest failures that God teaches us His greatest lessons. If you find yourself disappointed by a failure, look up to God and then back at the circumstances in which failure was victorious to see what lesson of value can be gained from it. Learn the lesson and your greatest success may be awaiting you just beyond your failure.
~ Christopher T. Ward
(An abandoned ranch house near Laurel, Montana - January 2005.)

BECAUSE OF THE LORD'S GREAT LOVE WE ARE NOT CONSUMED, FOR HIS COMPASSIONS NEVER FAIL. (LAMENTATIONS 3:22)

RELENTLESS AMBITIONS

Since late 2001, Jon Melby has been relentlessly pursuing his ambition of becoming a professional air-show pilot. With the support of his family and friends, Jon has turned his ambition into a success story. Jon flies the Pitts S1-11B high-performance aircraft. He has his ground-level waiver and more than 45 professional air-show performances to his name.
~ Christopher T. Ward
(Jon Melby pauses for a hang-ten while he prepares for his performance at the Copperstate Fly-in – October 2004.)

DO YOU SEE A MAN SKILLED IN HIS WORK? HE WILL SERVE BEFORE KINGS; HE WILL NOT SERVE BEFORE OBSCURE MEN. (PROVERBS 22:29)

OVERWHELMING LAZINESS

That's me lounging on the couch flipping through the channels while Taylor patiently waits for me to stop being lazy and take him to the skate park. Actually, I don't even own a television, but I couldn't find anyone who would agree to pose as the lazy dad for this photograph, so I volunteered myself. I will say, however, that I have had my fair share of laziness in life. Laziness can be a disease—don't let it keep you from accomplishing your dreams or spending quality time with your children.
~ Christopher T. Ward
(A lazy dad watches TV as his son waits for him – September 2005.)

LAZY PEOPLE WANT MUCH BUT GET LITTLE, BUT THOSE WHO WORK HARD WILL PROSPER AND BE SATISFIED.
(PROVERBS 13:4)

ONE TRUE LOVE

Many have been wrongfully deceived into believing that they can have true love if only they could find the right person. As marital strife and divorce devastate families and lives, we are left believing there is no such thing as true love. Don't let Satan lie to you. There is a love that never fails, and it is found solely in the Lord Jesus Christ. Where man has failed you, let God fill you. Ask God now to reveal His love for you and then follow His example.
~ Chawna Anderson
(The wedding rings of Ashley and Angus Scott sit on their wedding program prior to their ceremony - September 22, 2000.)

BUT THE EYES OF THE LORD ARE ON THOSE WHO FEAR HIM, ON THOSE WHOSE HOPE IS IN HIS UNFAILING LOVE.
(PSALM 33:18)

MANY HEARTBREAKS

The terrorist attacks of September 11 brought many heartbreaks to our country. It goes without saying that the events of that day changed our world, but perhaps nothing was changed more than the people of New York itself. Smoke still billowed from the ruins of the World Trade Center when I visited New York in late September 2001, and as I walked the streets of lower Manhattan, I could feel the effects of the shock wave that still rumbled within the people I encountered there. The heartbreak was very apparent in the presence of the people who had witnessed firsthand what most of us saw on a television screen. It was a much different city than the one I had experienced when I visited the year before. People were quiet, distant, and preoccupied by the unbelievable events of the previous weeks.
~ Christopher T. Ward
(People read messages left behind for the victims of the attacks on New York – September 2001.)

THE LORD WORKS RIGHTEOUSNESS AND JUSTICE FOR ALL THE OPPRESSED. (PSALM 103:6)

HEALTHIEST SATISFACTIONS

Do you have a passion that brings satisfaction to your life? A hobby such as fishing can be a great source of satisfaction. What gives you satisfaction? Passion for Christ will give you the great satisfaction of knowing that He gave his life for everything you do wrong on earth, no matter how costly a sin. Jesus' unconditional love is just that—unconditional.
~ Christopher T. Ward
(A fisherman fishes the waters of the Granite Reef Reservoir in Mesa, Arizona - 1995.)

THEN I REALIZED THAT IT IS GOOD AND PROPER FOR A MAN TO EAT AND DRINK, AND TO FIND SATISFACTION IN HIS TOILSOME LABOR UNDER THE SUN DURING THE FEW DAYS OF LIFE GOD HAS GIVEN HIM - FOR THIS IS HIS LOT.
(ECCLESIASTES 5:18)

Sickest Temptations

Do you have an addiction that tempts you? Addiction is sin. Pray to God to intervene and rid you of your addiction. With God's help there is no addiction that cannot be defeated. No addiction is more powerful than the sacrifice that Jesus made for you on the cross.
~ Christopher T. Ward
(This image was created for THE GREAT "I AM" - April 2004.)

No temptation has seized you except what is common to man. And God is faithful; he will not let you be tempted beyond what you can bear. But when you are tempted, he will also provide a way out so that you can stand up under it. (1 Corinthians 10:13)

Most Tender Healing

When you are wounded physically or emotionally and are in need of healing, the best thing you can do is ask God in prayer for His help and blessing.
~ Christopher T. Ward
(Carla Streng prepares to take the temperature of a woman of the Kangaonde Village in Malawi, Africa. Carla was one of 27 members of the missions team, put together by Canyon Ridge Bible Church, who traveled to Malawi on a missions trip in support of the African Bible College in Lilongwe – June 2004.)

He himself bore our sins in his body on the tree, so that we might die to sins and live for righteousness; by his wounds you have been healed. (1 Peter 2:24)

Meanest Illness

When John Hogue was just twenty years old he was diagnosed with cancer for the first time. I met John and his mother Judy during our missions trip to Malawi in 2004, and the love that they share was obvious during that trip. I would witness the great love that the Hogue family has for each other again when I was asked to accompany them to Cancún to photograph John's sister Courtney's wedding there.

At the age of twenty-four, John is once again faced with cancer. He is undergoing chemotherapy and fighting the disease with his faith as well as with a family that loves him dearly. It was hard for me to ask Judy if they would be willing to share their story in THE GREAT "I AM," but I knew that their testimony would touch so many people who may be going through similar circumstances. They agreed and I met John and Judy at Courtney's home to share the proof copy of the book and to take the photographs that I would need for their story. For the shoot, I asked John and Judy to sit together and read some of their favorite verses from the Bible. At first the mood was sullen and serious, but then in a gleaming instant the burden on their hearts was lifted away as John's smile beamed and Judy's love enveloped her son. At that moment, cancer's hold on the mood was defeated just as I snapped the shutter. This was the John and the Judy that I got to know in Africa, and I instantly knew I had the image I would need for the book. After showing Judy the image on my camera's monitor, I told her that it must be hard to smile like that during such a time, and Judy responded with this: "You have to smile on the good days, because the bad ones are unbearable."

Nowhere in the Bible does God promise us a life without difficulty or hardship. Jesus illustrates this when he comes across a man who was blind from birth. Jesus' disciples ask if the blindness is due to the man's sins or those of his parents. "Neither this man nor his parents sinned," said Jesus, "but this happened so that the work of God might be displayed in his life." (John 9:3 NIV) Jesus went on to heal the man of his blindness that day and the Glory of God was shown to the world.

After five sessions of chemotherapy and six weeks of radiation, John's current scans tell a similar story—no active signs of metastatic disease. Though John has been told that there is a 95% chance the disease will return, he lives on in faith, knowing that God is bigger than any 5% chance given by man. Is it "fair" that a 24-year-old should face cancer? No, but the Glory of God has been seen through John's remarkable headway against a disease that he was not expected to recover from.
~ Christopher T. Ward
(John and Judy Hogue for THE GREAT "I AM" - May 2005.)

See now that I myself am He! There is no god besides me. I put to death and I bring to life, I have wounded and I will heal, and no one can deliver out of my hand. (Deuteronomy 32:39)

ASTOUNDING COURAGE

Rock climbing requires courage, patience, knowledge, and endurance. Having faith in God requires similar skills. God is our rock, and walking daily with Him will build up our faith.
~ Chawna Anderson
(Taylor Ward ascends a rock face near Superior, Arizona – February 2005.)

BE ON YOUR GUARD; STAND FIRM IN THE FAITH; BE MEN OF COURAGE; BE STRONG. (1 CORINTHIANS 16:13)

DEVASTATING FEARS

Angelica Quiroz Popoca was born sixteen weeks premature and weighed only one pound, four ounces. Her mother, Marisol, went into the hospital twenty weeks pregnant and stayed on complete bed rest until Angelica was born four weeks later. When Marisol was no longer able to hold the baby and was forced to deliver, the doctors asked her and her husband Pedro, a very difficult question. "Would you like us to lay the baby on your chest and you hold her until she dies, or shall we put her in the NICU and pray she survives?" Obviously Marisol and Pedro believed in prayer. They have faced many fearful times since Angelica's birth, the worst being the insertion of the tracheostomy tube. Through it all, Marisol decided to stand on what God told her and not on what she heard from the doctors. Angelica is now an extremely active child who loves to play with her big sister Edith. She is soon to be scheduled to have her tracheostomy tube removed and to begin preschool. Pedro works very hard providing for his family, and Marisol is a family advisor volunteer at the children's hospital helping other parents facing difficult situations.
~ Chawna Anderson
(Marisol Popoca swings her daughter Angelica in this photo created for THE GREAT "I AM" - September 2005.)

SO DO NOT FEAR, FOR I AM WITH YOU; DO NOT BE DISMAYED, FOR I AM YOUR GOD. I WILL STRENGTHEN YOU AND HELP YOU; I WILL UPHOLD YOU WITH MY RIGHTEOUS RIGHT HAND. (ISAIAH 41:10)

IMPOSSIBLE DREAMS

Do you have a dream that seems impossible or out of reach? Since I can remember, I've wanted to be a pilot, but making that dream a reality has eluded me so far. Or is it I who has eluded the dream? If we let them, life's details can get in the way of our greatest desires.
~ Christopher T. Ward
(Taylor Ward watches on as two planes take off during an air show at Williams Field, Mesa, Arizona – 1995.)

MAY HE GIVE YOU THE DESIRE OF YOUR HEART AND MAKE ALL YOUR PLANS SUCCEED. (PSALM 20:4)

UNFULFILLED EXPECTATIONS

My husband, Jeremiah, our son, Ian, and I have had to face many challenges. We have had to overcome some pretty tough emotional, physical, financial, and spiritual battles in our lifetime. God has never once left us or forsaken us. No matter what we were going through, our fault or not, He has never changed. He continues to love and comfort us with open arms. He is a God who is true to His word and never breaks a promise. I guarantee you, if God was ever going to give up on anyone, it would have been us. Yet He always remains the same: yesterday, today, and forever.
~ Chawna Anderson
(The Anderson family in their home in Glendale, Arizona – August 2005.)

THEY CRIED TO YOU AND WERE SAVED; IN YOU THEY TRUSTED AND WERE NOT DISAPPOINTED. (PSALM 22:5)

GUIDING LIGHT

The word of God is the guiding light that will lead you away from the rocks when you find yourself in the middle of one of life's storms. Make it a habit to read the word daily and make time for God.
~ Christopher T. Ward
(The sun sets at the Nobska Lighthouse near Falmouth, Massachusetts – October 2001.)

"ARISE, SHINE, FOR YOUR LIGHT HAS COME, AND THE GLORY OF THE LORD RISES UPON YOU. SEE, DARKNESS COVERS THE EARTH AND THICK DARKNESS IS OVER THE PEOPLES, BUT THE LORD RISES UPON YOU AND HIS GLORY APPEARS OVER YOU. (ISAIAH 60:1-2)

CONSUMING DARKNESS

I took this photograph of little Wongani Shumba the morning I was to return to the States from Malawi in 2004. He was taken in by the African Bible College (ABC) Medical Clinic at the age of two-and-a-half after Nancy's Missionary could no longer care for him. Nancy's Missionary took him in after he was abandoned by his aunt and grandmother at the Nkhoma village in Malawi. When Wongani came to the ABC, he was so malnourished and weak that he could not move. In just six short months, Wongani would take his first steps on the ABC campus at the age of three. The three candles in the photograph represent his mother, his father, and his identical twin brother, who have all died as a result of AIDS. Wongani has tested negative for HIV.
~ Christopher T. Ward
(Wongani Shumba stands in front of candles representing his family - June 2004.)

YOU ARE MY LAMP, O LORD; THE LORD TURNS MY DARKNESS INTO LIGHT. WITH YOUR HELP I CAN ADVANCE AGAINST A TROOP; WITH MY GOD I CAN SCALE A WALL. (2 SAMUEL 22:29-30)

THRILLING EXCITEMENT

There aren't many things more exciting than aerobatics! Jon Melby travels the country on the air-show circuit performing in his new Pitts S-1-11B. How exciting is that?
~ Christopher T. Ward
(This photo was taken for Jon Melby Airshow's 2004 marketing campaign and used in his business cards, brochures, and other marketing items - Chandler, Arizona - August 2004.)

REJOICE IN THE LORD ALWAYS. I WILL SAY IT AGAIN: REJOICE! (PHILIPPIANS 4:4)

TEDIOUS BOREDOM

The next time you find yourself overwhelmed by boredom or a loss of direction in your life, open the Bible and read, for the word of God is great in its inspiration for those who will listen.
~ Christopher T. Ward
(Taylor Ward does his best to look bored in this photograph - May 2003.)

SOW YOUR SEED IN THE MORNING, AND AT EVENING LET NOT YOUR HANDS BE IDLE, FOR YOU DO NOT KNOW WHICH WILL SUCCEED, WHETHER THIS OR THAT, OR WHETHER BOTH WILL DO EQUALLY WELL. (ECCLESIASTES 11:6)

PUREST CLEANSING

In May 2005, I traveled to Uganda, Africa, to help with the construction of the newest African Bible College campus being built in Kampala. Many of the workers with whom I worked closely on the campus became my friends, and in this series of photographs, my friend David Kalega is baptized by my friends Don Richard Ebiju (holding Bible) and Alex Kikumu. All three men are local Ugandans who work on the construction team building the ABC campus. David is a painter, Richard is the lead carpenter, and Alex is the campus welder and fabricator. The ceremony took place at sunset at Lake Victoria, the second largest body of fresh water in the world and the source of the river Nile.
~ Christopher T. Ward
(David Kalega is baptized by Alex Kikumu and Richard Ebiju in Lake Victoria, Uganda, Africa – June 2005.)

I WILL SPRINKLE CLEAN WATER ON YOU, AND YOU WILL BE CLEAN; I WILL CLEANSE YOU FROM ALL YOUR IMPURITIES AND FROM ALL YOUR IDOLS. (EZEKIEL 36:25)

WORRISOME JUNK

We often hold on to things that, in reality, we will never use again but which we think we might need later. After years of collecting such things, we may find they have become a worrisome burden that is not easy to dispose of. When I visited New York in September 2000, the garbage strike was in full swing, and trash was piling up on the city streets.
~ Christopher T. Ward
(A huge pile of trash sits on a New York City street – September 2000.)

THEREFORE DO NOT WORRY ABOUT TOMORROW, FOR TOMORROW WILL WORRY ABOUT ITSELF. EACH DAY HAS ENOUGH TROUBLE OF ITS OWN. (MATTHEW 6:34)

WISEST CHOICE

On two of my missions trips to Africa, I brought with me cases of pocket Bibles to hand out to the people that I met. During my trip to Malawi, I visited Lake Malawi near Salima and gave out Bibles to men who were carving "curios," the Malawian name for souvenirs. In my own Bible, I keep several pressed poppies from a road trip to Montana I made with my father in 1998. I now use them as place markers for some of my favorite scriptures. Grant Chande, one of the men that I spoke to, would not stop asking for one of my bookmarks to go with the Bible I had given him. I obliged and he now has a bible and a very special bookmark.
~ Christopher T. Ward
(Grant Chande of Salima, Malawi, Africa, holds a pressed Montana poppy used as a bookmark while reading from the book of John – June 2004.)

THIS DAY I CALL HEAVEN AND EARTH AS WITNESSES AGAINST YOU THAT I HAVE SET BEFORE YOU LIFE AND DEATH, BLESSINGS AND CURSES. NOW CHOOSE LIFE, SO THAT YOU AND YOUR CHILDREN MAY LIVE (DEUTERONOMY 30:19)

SILLIEST MISTAKE

We often make silly mistakes, but our biggest ones are usually born out of sin. This photograph is of an accident that I happened upon, and as it turned out, the occupants had stolen the vehicle and were running from police when the driver lost control and rammed the light pole. Neither of the occupants was injured in their folly, and in fact, both fled the scene on foot to avoid capture.
~ Christopher T. Ward
(A stolen vehicle sits overturned after its thief lost control during a police pursuit - August 1997.)

FOR THE FOOLISHNESS OF GOD IS WISER THAN MAN'S WISDOM, AND THE WEAKNESS OF GOD IS STRONGER THAN MAN'S STRENGTH. BROTHERS, THINK OF WHAT YOU WERE WHEN YOU WERE CALLED. NOT MANY OF YOU WERE WISE BY HUMAN STANDARDS; NOT MANY WERE INFLUENTIAL; NOT MANY WERE OF NOBLE BIRTH. BUT GOD CHOSE THE FOOLISH THINGS OF THE WORLD TO SHAME THE WISE; GOD CHOSE THE WEAK THINGS OF THE WORLD TO SHAME THE STRONG. (1 CORINTHIANS 1:25-27)

ABUNDANT FORGIVENESS

When you think you've gone beyond the threshold of God's love and forgiveness, take a moment to remind yourself that Jesus Christ, whose unconditional love is everlasting, chose to die for each and every one of our sins, no matter how complex. When all seems lost, remember this: *"for all have sinned and fall short of the glory of God, and are justified freely by his grace through the redemption that came by Christ Jesus."*[38]
~ Christopher T. Ward
(Three large crosses constructed for this photograph stand in the desert near Scottsdale, Arizona - March 2004.)

THEY REFUSED TO LISTEN AND FAILED TO REMEMBER THE MIRACLES YOU PERFORMED AMONG THEM. THEY BECAME STIFF-NECKED AND IN THEIR REBELLION APPOINTED A LEADER IN ORDER TO RETURN TO THEIR SLAVERY. BUT YOU ARE A FORGIVING GOD, GRACIOUS AND COMPASSIONATE, SLOW TO ANGER AND ABOUNDING IN LOVE. THEREFORE YOU DID NOT DESERT THEM. (NEHEMIAH 9:17)

ENDLESS SINS

As Christians we have all turned from God or stumbled during our Christian walk. When you stumble, thank God for His forgiveness, for Jesus Christ gave His life for the forgiveness of our sins. Though we may be disciplined by the hand of God for our shortcomings, we must remember that it is for our good. For as a child is disciplined by his father out of love so are we disciplined by our Heavenly Father.
~ Christopher T. Ward
(An inmate of the Maricopa County Jail sits behind bars in this photograph taken for *THE GREAT "I AM"* in 2003.)

"I HAVE NOT COME TO CALL THE RIGHTEOUS, BUT SINNERS TO REPENTANCE." (LUKE 5:32)

JESUS REPLIED, "I TELL YOU THE TRUTH, EVERYONE WHO SINS IS A SLAVE TO SIN. NOW A SLAVE HAS NO PERMANENT PLACE IN THE FAMILY, BUT A SON BELONGS TO IT FOREVER. SO IF THE SON SETS YOU FREE, YOU WILL BE FREE INDEED." (JOHN 8:34-36)

TRUST ME

Lift up your problems to God, and trust in Him to provide the solutions to your greatest problems, for His power and might are without boundaries. With God nothing is impossible.
~ Christopher T. Ward
(My good friends Jeremy and Brooks Wolfe share the Bible with their son, Connor, and daughter, Kayla - September 2005.)

TRUST IN THE LORD WITH ALL YOUR HEART AND LEAN NOT ON YOUR OWN UNDERSTANDING; IN ALL YOUR WAYS ACKNOWLEDGE HIM, AND HE WILL MAKE YOUR PATHS STRAIGHT. (PROVERBS 3:5-6)

I LOVE AND RESPECT YOU DEEPLY

Each and every one of us stumbles, falls, and fails while learning to walk. But have faith! For Jesus' love is infinite and real, and his forgiveness is abundant.
~ Christopher T. Ward
(My good friends Jeremy and Brooks Wolfe run through a pistachio-tree grove in Chandler, Arizona – January 2004.)

FOR I AM CONVINCED THAT NEITHER DEATH NOR LIFE, NEITHER ANGELS NOR DEMONS, NEITHER THE PRESENT NOR THE FUTURE, NOR ANY POWERS, NEITHER HEIGHT NOR DEPTH, NOR ANYTHING ELSE IN ALL CREATION, WILL BE ABLE TO SEPARATE US FROM THE LOVE OF GOD THAT IS IN CHRIST JESUS OUR LORD. (ROMANS 8:38-39)

What about you?

Jesus asks the most important question you will ever answer. Recently, I had a discussion with an agnostic acquaintance in which he told me that there are going to be a lot of disappointed people who, after they die, find out there is no God. The rest of the day his comments rang in my ears until that evening I had a revelation. My thought was simple yet mind-blowing, and it was "how much more disappointing it would be to spend an eternity wishing you had answered Jesus' question correctly!" How will you answer Jesus' question?
~Christopher T. Ward
(This photograph was created with the help of Pastor Andy Welch for *THE GREAT "I AM"* – June 2003.)

He replied, "Because you have so little faith. I tell you the truth, if you have faith as small as a mustard seed, you can say to this mountain, 'Move from here to there' and it will move. Nothing will be impossible for you." (Matthew 17:20)

Prayer of Acceptance

My friend Irving Mawolo bows his head in prayer for this photograph for THE GREAT "I AM." After graduating from high school in 1985, Irving was accepted to attend the first African Bible College that was founded and built by Nel and Jack Chinchen in Liberia in 1976. In 1989, civil war broke out in Liberia, and Irving was forced to flee by foot to Sierra Leone, leaving his entire family and all of his possessions behind.

Irving stayed in Freetown, Sierra Leone, for three years until his sister sent for him from Abidjan, Ivory Coast. Once there, Irving worked for Cumberland Presbyterian Church as an assistant pastor. In 1995, the Chinchens visited Ivory Coast to graduate the students who had fled there because of the war in Liberia. In 1997, Irving moved from Ivory Coast to Malawi, where he would work closely with the Chinchens as an administrative assistant and head of the sports program on the ABC campus.

In 2000, Irving came to the U.S. to attend Southern California Bible College and Seminary in San Diego, where he completed his master's degree in Biblical Studies in 2002. Upon graduating, Irving traveled back to Malawi, where he served as chaplain and dean of men and taught Bibliology at the African Bible College. I met and became good friends with Irving in 2004 when I roomed with him at the African Bible College, during my missions trip there.

In 2005, I find myself returning the favor as Irving has come to stay with me in Chandler, Arizona. He is now attending Phoenix Seminary School in Scottsdale, where he is studying for his Master of Divinity degree. Irving's long-term goal is to eventually return to his home country of Liberia to do what he can to bring peace and stability to a nation that has been ravaged by 15 years of civil war and unrest.
~ Christopher T. Ward
(Irving Mawolo poses for this portrait of prayer – October 2005.)

But if from there you seek the LORD your God, you will find him if you look for him with all your heart and with all your soul. (Deuteronomy 4:29)

Baptism Series

Baptism is a very important step in our Christian walk. It was Peter who said, "'Repent and be baptized, every one of you, in the name of Jesus Christ for the forgiveness of your sins. And you will receive the gift of the Holy Spirit."[39] Baptism is a step that brings us closer to God through the pledge of a good conscience toward Him.
~ Christopher T. Ward
(David Kalega is baptized by Alex Kikumu and Richard Ebiju in Lake Victoria, Uganda, Africa – June 2005.)

"And now what are you waiting for? Get up, be baptized and wash your sins away, calling on his name." (Acts 22:16)

Fishers of men

This image was captured during my trip to Uganda. To capture this image, I traveled by boat from Jinja, Uganda, up the Nile River into Lake Victoria, where I photographed native fishermen fishing its waters for tilapia - the staple source of meat there. Fishing is one of the largest trades along the banks of Lake Victoria and a large part of the economy of the region.
~ Christopher T. Ward
(Ugandan fishermen fish the waters of Lake Victoria, Uganda – June 2005.)

As Jesus was walking beside the Sea of Galilee, he saw two brothers, Simon called Peter and his brother Andrew. They were casting a net into the lake, for they were fishermen. "Come, follow me", Jesus said, "and I will make you fishers of men." At once they left their nets and followed him. (Matthew 4:18-20)

FINDING PURPOSE

Chawna and I have both been involved in missions work and other ministries both locally and abroad. Unfortunately, raising money is a largely unseen, seldom-thought-of reality of the work that goes into successful missions trips. It is one of the largest challenges that Christians who are involved in Christian ministry face today. When I went on my first missions trip to Malawi in 2004, I was faced with that very challenge: raising funds to cover such things as shots and inoculations, passport expenses, specialty items and clothing, as well as very expensive airfare to my destination in Africa. I am blessed to have had family and friends who were willing to help make my missions trip a reality by their response to a letter I wrote asking for their support. However, I honestly felt kind of awkward asking people for money with nothing to give in return for their generous gifts beyond the stories of my awesome experiences in Africa. It just didn't "feel" right. Well, Scripture says many are the plans in a man's heart, but it is the LORD'S purpose that prevails.[40] After three missions to Africa, I am now clear about what that purpose has become. Chawna and I made the connection that THE GREAT "I AM" would be a GREAT tool that Christians involved in missions or other ministries could use to help raise support money for their own missions and ministries across the globe. It is our hope that THE GREAT "I AM" can benefit ministries and the missions community not only by helping Christians raise money for ministries through the sale of this book but also by using it as a vehicle to illustrate simply, through stories and photographs, the message we as Christians are called upon to spread to the ends of the earth.

It is our aim to ease the burden of fund-raising for ministries and missions by providing to churches, missions organizations, and outreach ministries THE GREAT "I AM" at a generously discounted bulk rate specifically for this purpose—to give donors something in return for their gracious gifts and to spread the word of Jesus Christ. If you are interested in using THE GREAT "I AM" to help make your ministry a reality, please take a look at our Web site www.thegreat-iam.com for information on how we can help you achieve your fund-raising goals.

THE GREAT "I AM" makes a wonderful gift for believers and nonbelievers alike. Receive $5.00 off the retail price when you order The Great "I AM" from the official Web site.

THE GREAT "I AM" also makes an amazing outreach ministry and fund-raising tool for churches, ministries, and missions organizations. We are offering special discounts for outreach ministries, book stores, and missions organizations who are interested in purchasing THE GREAT "I AM" in bulk. Please visit our Web site for more details.

THE GREAT "I AM" can be ordered from the Web site, where we have provided a secure shopping-cart for your on-line ordering convenience.

Share your story! Share with us how THE GREAT "I AM" helped launch your ministry or helped you reach someone who was lost. Email us at testimony@thegreat-iam.com and your story could show up on THE GREAT "I AM" Web site!

WWW.THEGREAT-IAM.COM

FOOTNOTES:

1.
God said to Moses, "I am who I am. This is what you are to say to the Israelites: 'I AM has sent me to you.'"

2.
I cried out to God for help; I cried out to God to hear me.

3. Psalm 63:1 (NIV)
O God, you are my God, earnestly I seek you; my soul thirsts for you, my body longs for you, in a dry and weary land where there is no water.

4. Psalm 120:1 (NIV)
I call on the LORD in my distress, and he answers me.

5. Hosea 2:14 (NIV)
Therefore I am now going to allure her; I will lead her into the desert and speak tenderly to her.

6. John 14:6 (NIV)
Jesus answered, "I am the way and the truth and the life. No one comes to the Father except through me."

7. John 8:12 (NIV)
When Jesus spoke again to the people, he said, "I am the light of the world. Whoever follows me will never walk in darkness, but will have the light of life."

8. John 6:35 (NIV)
Then Jesus declared, "I am the bread of life. He who comes to me will never go hungry, and he who believes in me will never be thirsty."

9. Isaiah 44:6 (NIV)
This is what the LORD says— Israel's King and Redeemer, the LORD Almighty: I am the first and I am the last; apart from me there is no God.

10. John 10:11 (NIV)
"I am the good shepherd. The good shepherd lays down his life for the sheep."

11. Exodus 3:14 (NIV)
God said to Moses, "I am who I am. This is what you are to say to the Israelites: 'I AM has sent me to you.'"

12. Jeremiah 29:11 (NIV)
"For I know the plans I have for you," declares the LORD, "plans to prosper you and not to harm you, plans to give you hope and a future."

13. Isaiah 43:1 (NLT)
But now, O Israel, the LORD who created you says: "Do not be afraid, for I have ransomed you. I have called you by name; you are mine."

14. Jeremiah 1:5 (NIV)
Before I formed you in the womb I knew you, before you were born I set you apart; I appointed you as a prophet to the nations.

15. John 15:5 (NIV)
"I am the vine; you are the branches. If a man remains in me and I in him, he will bear much fruit; apart from me you can do nothing."

16. John 15:16 (NIV)
"You did not choose me, but I chose you and appointed you to go and bear fruit—fruit that will last. Then the Father will give you whatever you ask in my name."

17. John 15:9 (NIV)
"As the Father has loved me, so have I loved you. Now remain in my love."

18. Matthew 28:20 (NIV)
"[A]nd teaching them to obey everything I have commanded you. And surely I am with you always, to the very end of the age."

19. Isaiah 65:1 (NIV)
I revealed myself to those who did not ask for me; I was found by those who did not seek me. To a nation that did not call on my name, I said, "Here am I, here am I."

20. Matthew 18:20 (NIV)
"For where two or three come together in my name, there am I with them."

21. Jeremiah 29:13-14 (NIV)
"You will seek me and find me when you seek me with all your heart."[13] I will be found by you," declares the LORD, "and will bring you back from captivity. I will gather you from all the nations and places where I have banished you," declares the LORD, "and will bring you back to the place from which I carried you into exile."[14]

22. John 14:20 (NIV)
"On that day you will realize that I am in my Father, and you are in me, and I am in you."

23. Isaiah 58:9 (NIV)
Then you will call, and the LORD will answer; you will cry for help, and he will say: "Here am I." If you do away with the yoke of oppression, with the pointing finger and malicious talk, … ."

24. Jeremiah 32:27 (NIV)
"I am the LORD, the God of all mankind. Is anything too hard for me?"

25. Isaiah 41:10 (NIV)
"So do not fear, for I am with you; do not be dismayed, for I am your God. I will strengthen you and help you; I will uphold you with my righteous right hand."

26. John 11:25 (NIV)
Jesus said to her, "I am the resurrection and the life. He who believes in me will live, even though he dies."

27. Mark 5:36 (NIV)
Ignoring what they said, Jesus told the synagogue ruler, "Don't be afraid; just believe."

28. John 21:16 (NIV)
Again Jesus said, "Simon son of John, do you truly love me?" He answered, "Yes, Lord, you know that I love you." Jesus said, "Take care of my sheep."

29. Matthew 9:2,22 (NIV)
Some men brought to him a paralytic, lying on a mat. When Jesus saw their faith, he said to the paralytic, "Take heart, son; your sins are forgiven." (9:2)
Jesus turned and saw her. "Take heart, daughter," he said, "your faith has healed you." And the woman was healed from that moment. (9:22)

30. Malachi 1:2 (NIV)
"I have loved you," says the LORD. "But you ask, 'How have you loved us?' Was not Esau Jacob's brother?" the LORD says. "Yet I have loved Jacob."

31. Isaiah 48:17 (NIV)
This is what the LORD says— your Redeemer, the Holy One of Israel: "I am the LORD your God, who teaches you what is best for you, who directs you in the way you should go."

32. Jeremiah 30:11 (NIV)
"I am with you and will save you," declares the LORD. "Though I completely destroy all the nations among which I scatter you, I will not completely destroy you. I will discipline you but only with justice; I will not let you go entirely unpunished."

33. Matthew 6:25 (NIV)
"Therefore I tell you, do not worry about your life, what you will eat or drink; or about your body, what you will wear. Is not life more important than food, and the body more important than clothes?"

34. Matthew 7:7 (NIV)
"Ask and it will be given to you; seek and you will find; knock and the door will be opened to you."

35. Jeremiah 31:3 (NIV)
The LORD appeared to us in the past, saying: "I have loved you with an everlasting love; I have drawn you with loving-kindness."

36. Jeremiah 30:17 (NIV)
"But I will restore you to health and heal your wounds," declares the LORD, "because you are called an outcast, Zion for whom no one cares."

37. Jeremiah 30:22 (NIV)
"So you will be my people, and I will be your God."

38. Romans 3:23-24 (NIV)
[F]or all have sinned and fall short of the glory of God,[23] and are justified freely by his grace through the redemption that came by Christ Jesus.[24]

39. Acts 2:38 (NIV)
Peter replied, "Repent and be baptized, every one of you, in the name of Jesus Christ for the forgiveness of your sins. And you will receive the gift of the Holy Spirit."

40. Proverbs 19:21 (NIV)
Many are the plans in a man's heart, but it is the LORD's purpose that prevails.